ILLUSTRATED BIOGRAPHY FOR KIDS
ALBERT EINSTEIN
EXTRAORDINARY SCIENTIST
WHO CHANGED THE WORLD

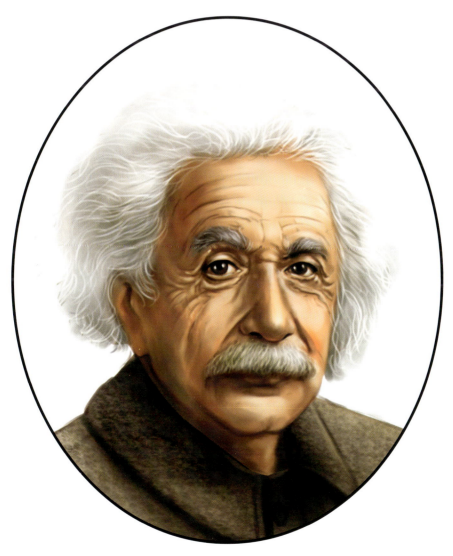

Wonder House

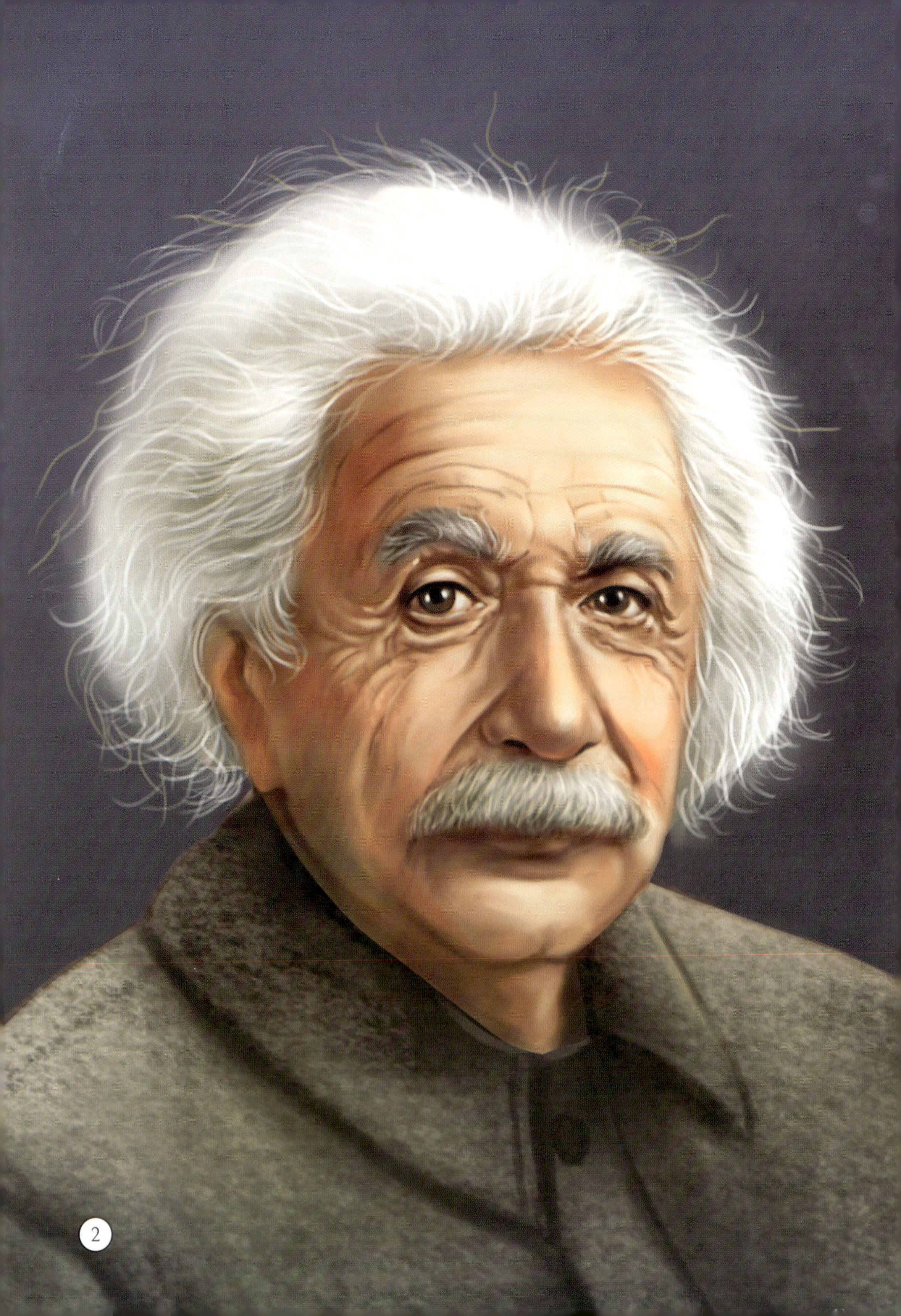

QUINTESSENTIALLY GENIUS

Albert Einstein has been widely acknowledged as one of the greatest minds of the twentieth century. He was born in Germany and is known as the world's most famous theoretical physicist. He is best known for his work in the development of general and special theories of relativity, quantum mechanics, photoelectric effect, explanation of Brownian motion, and for his most famous equation of mass-energy equivalence. His contribution in modern physics is undeniable. He received the Nobel Prize in 1921, for his discovery of photoelectric effect and in making significant contribution in the field of theoretical physics. There is even an element named Einsteinium named after him in the periodic table.

CURIOSITY IS THE KEY

Einstein was born in Ulm, Germany, on 14 March 1879. His father was Hermann Einstein, a salesman and his mother Pauline Koch ran the household. In his early years, he became fascinated with the magnetic compass. From his first encounter with the instrument, he was dazzled with the invisible forces that led to the deflection of its needles. He was fascinated with the studies of science and mathematics to such an extent that in no time the geometrical concepts were on his tips.

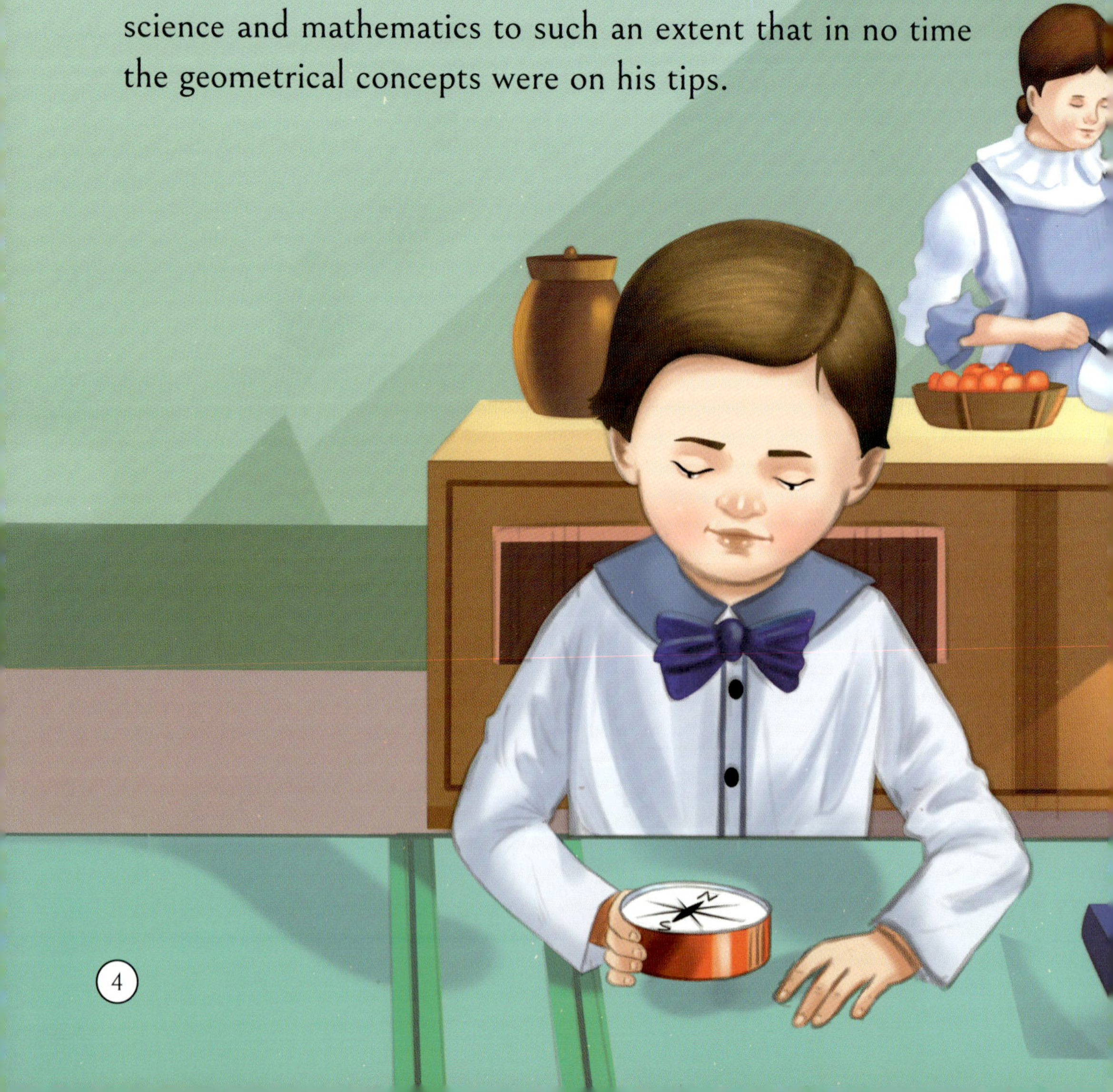

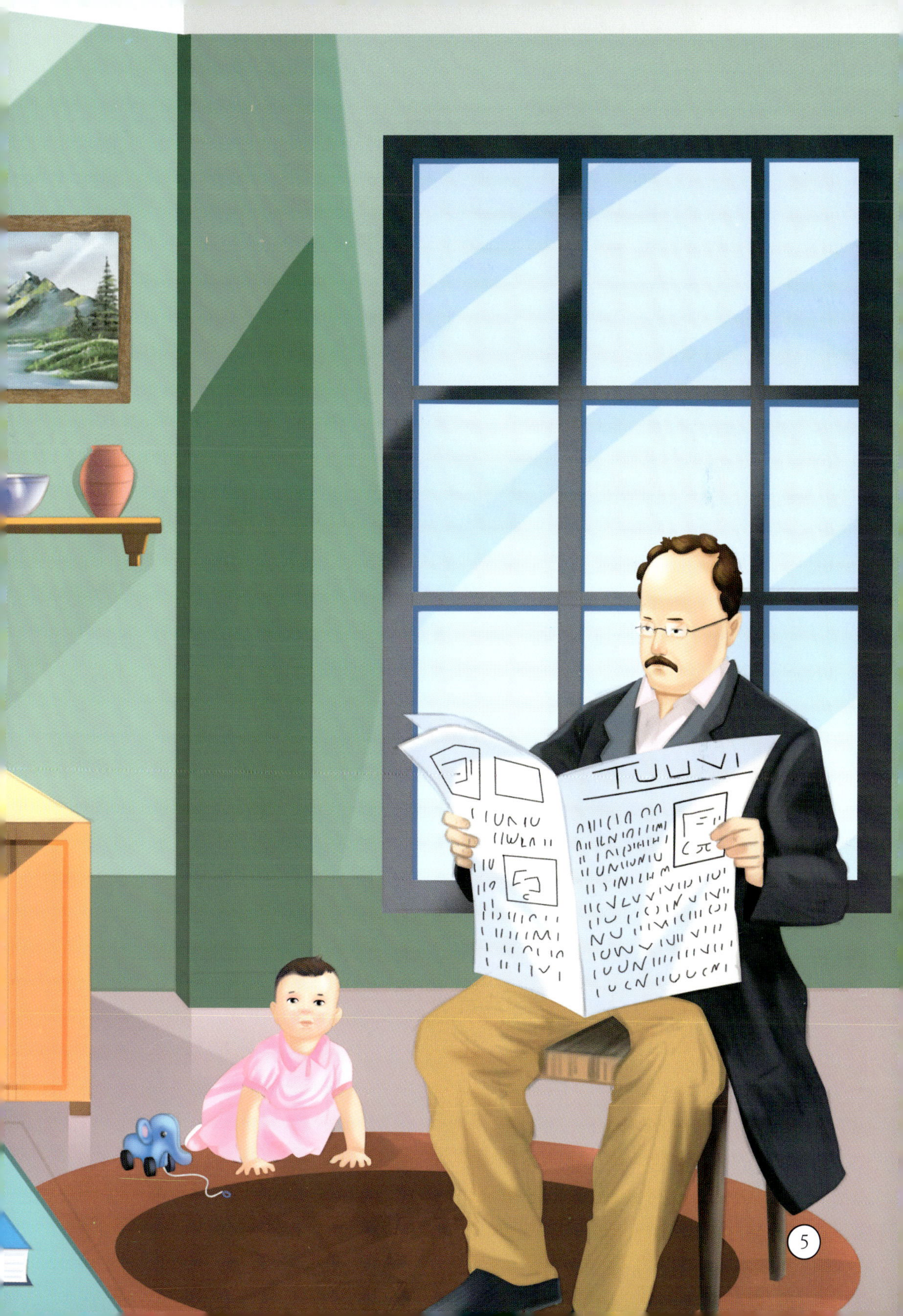

CHILD PRODIGY

Einstein was stupefied with the geometrical concepts and excelled them in no time. He learned calculus and mastered both differential and integral calculus by the age of 14. He devoted himself to the studies of mathematics with such vigor that he was convinced that all the concepts in the universe can be explained with the help of mathematics.

At the age of 13, Einstein indulged in the studies of philosophy, he in no time finished Immanuel Kant's *Critique of Pure Reason* and he became his favorite philosopher. His tutor was amazed by his ingenuity; how a mere child can study and understand such difficult works of philosophy which are incomprehensible to even young adults.

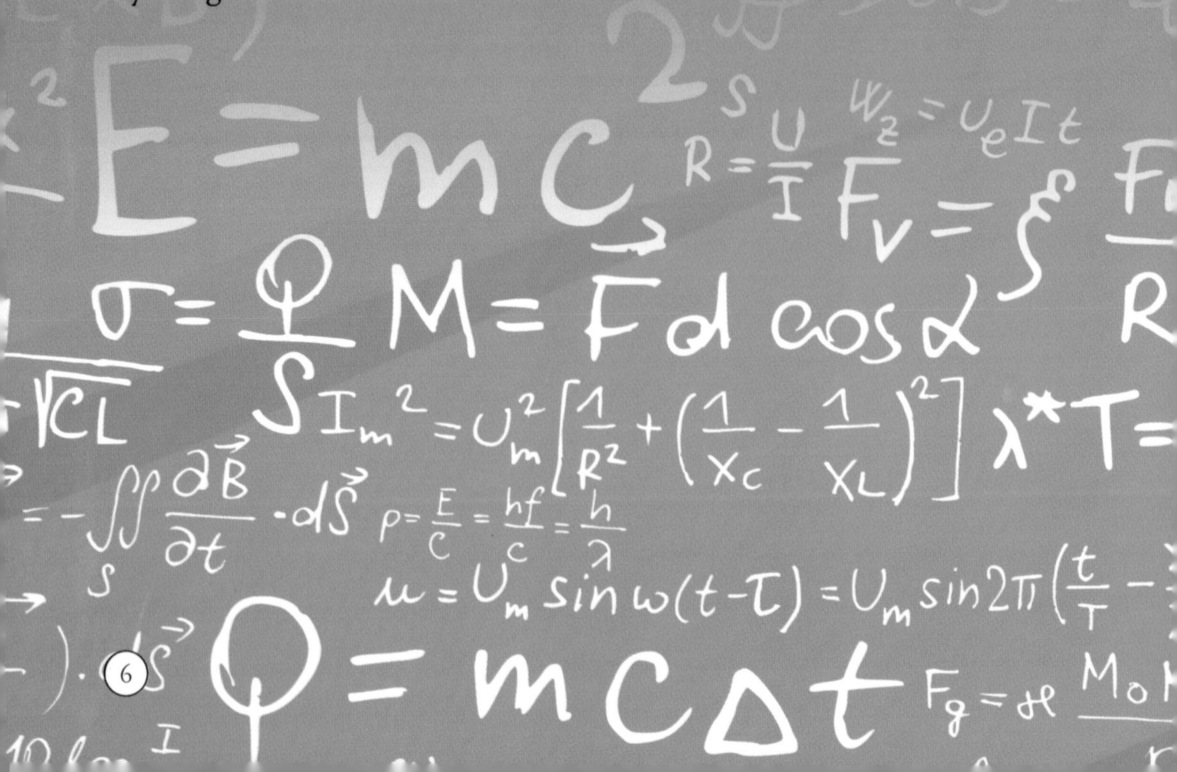
E=mc2
R=U/I
M=Fd cos α
Q=mcΔt

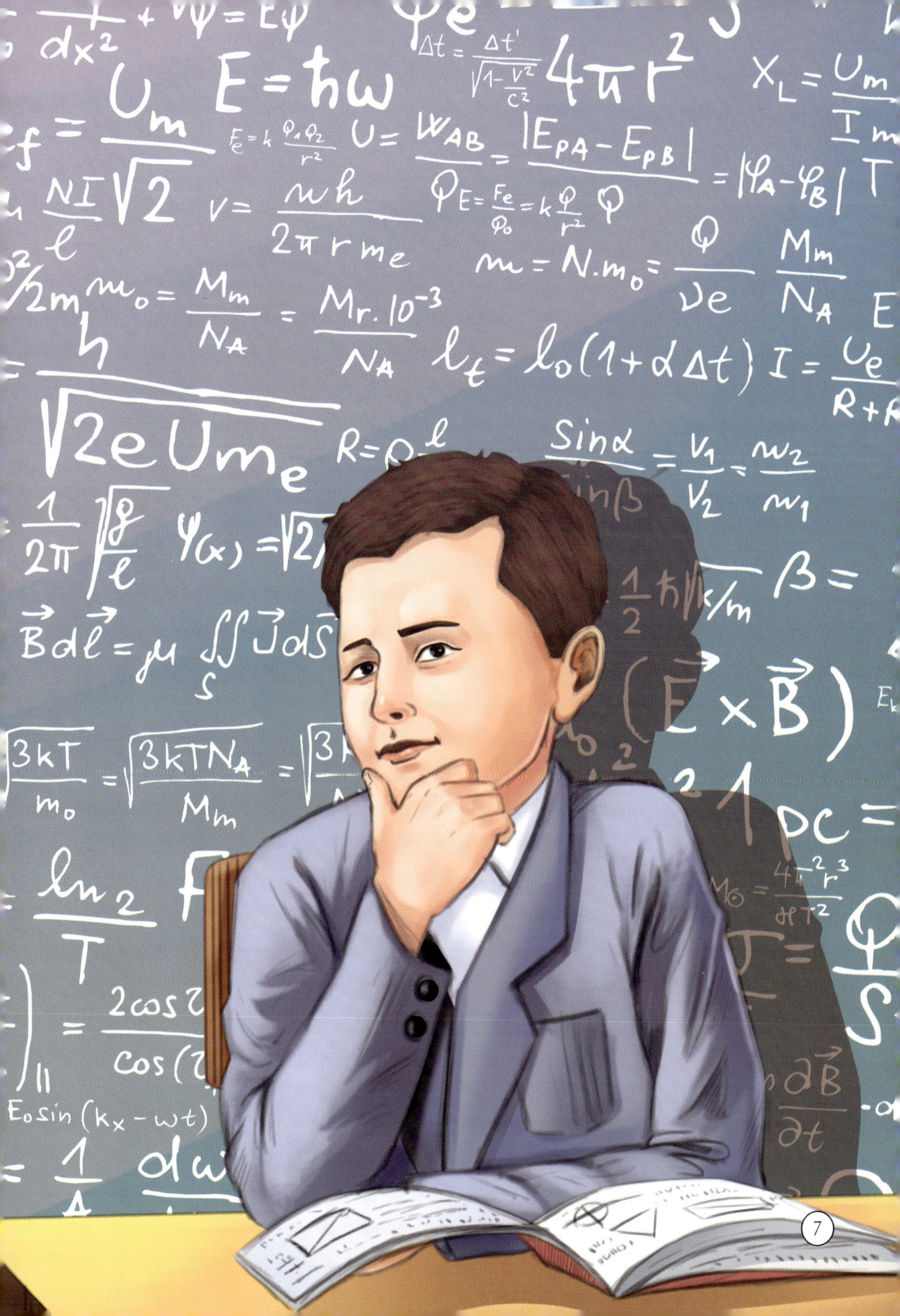

$E = \hbar\omega$
$4\pi r^2$
$m = N.m_0$
$l_t = l_0(1+\alpha\Delta t)$
$\sqrt{2eUm_e}$
$E_0 \sin(kx - \omega t)$
$(E \times B)$

Einstein started his early education at Luitpold-Gymnasium, later renamed after his own name as—Albert-Einstein-Gymnasium. During 1894, his father's company lost a bid to supply electricity to Munich. This huge loss in business forced the sale of the company

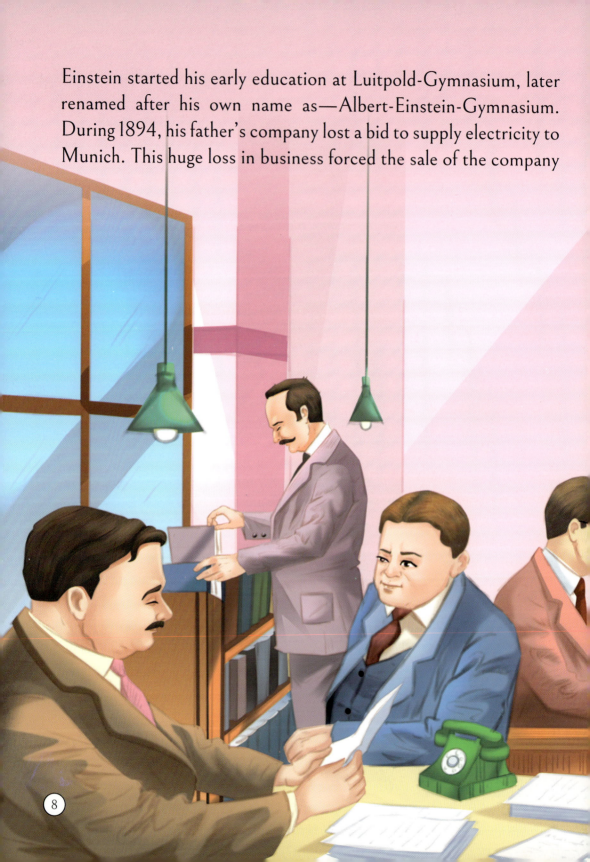

and compelled the family to move to Italy in search for business. Einstein completed his primary and secondary school education in Germany and later left to join his family back in Italy.

In 1896, he entered the Swiss Federal Polytechnic School in Zurich to be trained as a teacher in physics and mathematics. Here he met his future wife, Mileva Maric, who was the only woman in the physics and mathematics department of his course.

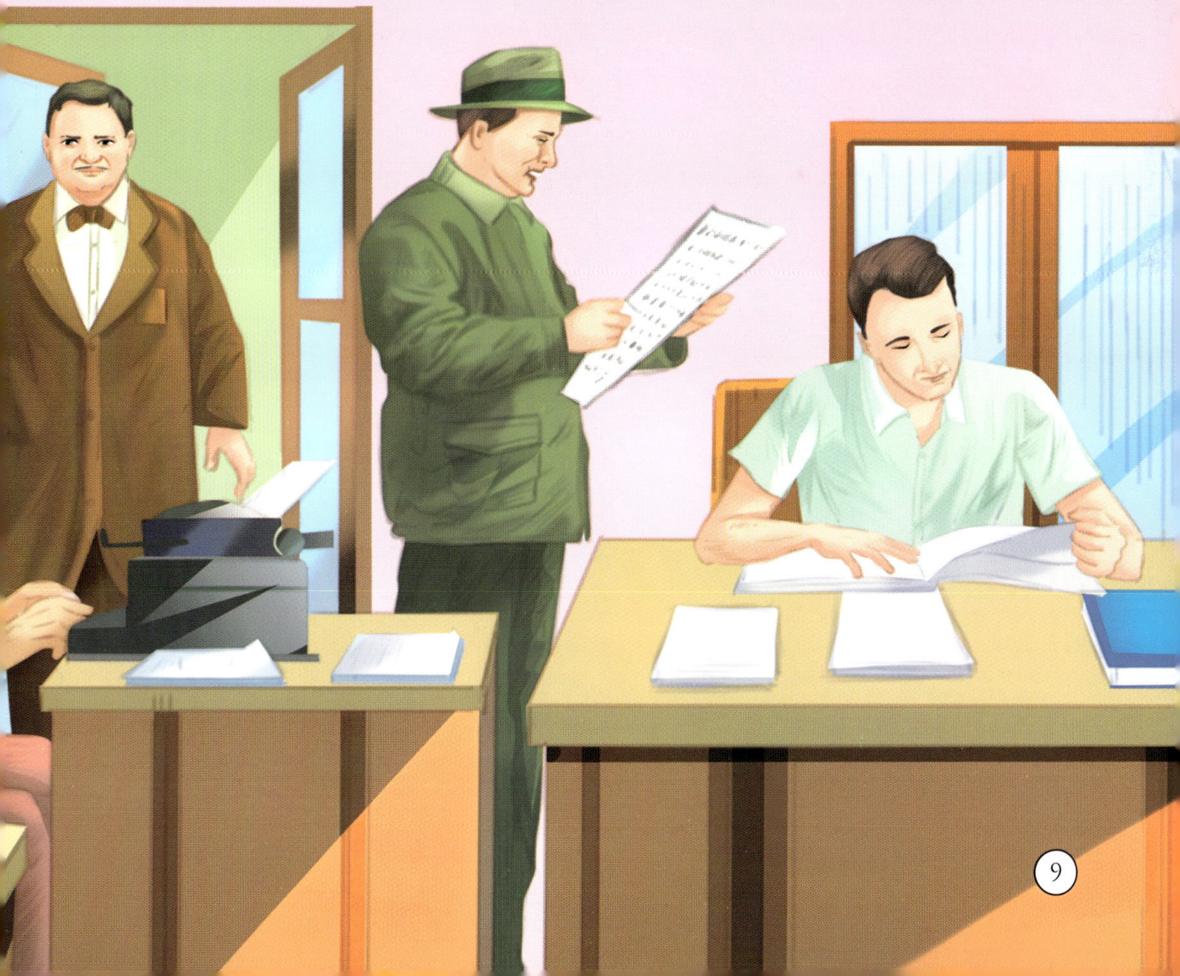

NEW BEGINNINGS

In 1901, Einstein acquired Swiss citizenship and was awarded the Federal teaching diploma. But unfortunately, even after successfully completing his course, he could not acquire a single academic position. Later Einstein secured a job as a technical assistant at the Swiss Patent Office. With a small yet a steady income, Einstein married Maric, on 6 January 1903. Their children, Hans Albert and Eduard, were born in 1904 and 1910, respectively.

Einstein's time at the patent office was very productive, not only did he learn a great deal about machine technology, but it also gave him enough time to find answers to the queries regarding the nature of light and the fundamental connection between space and time. The glimpse of which could be seen in his later works.

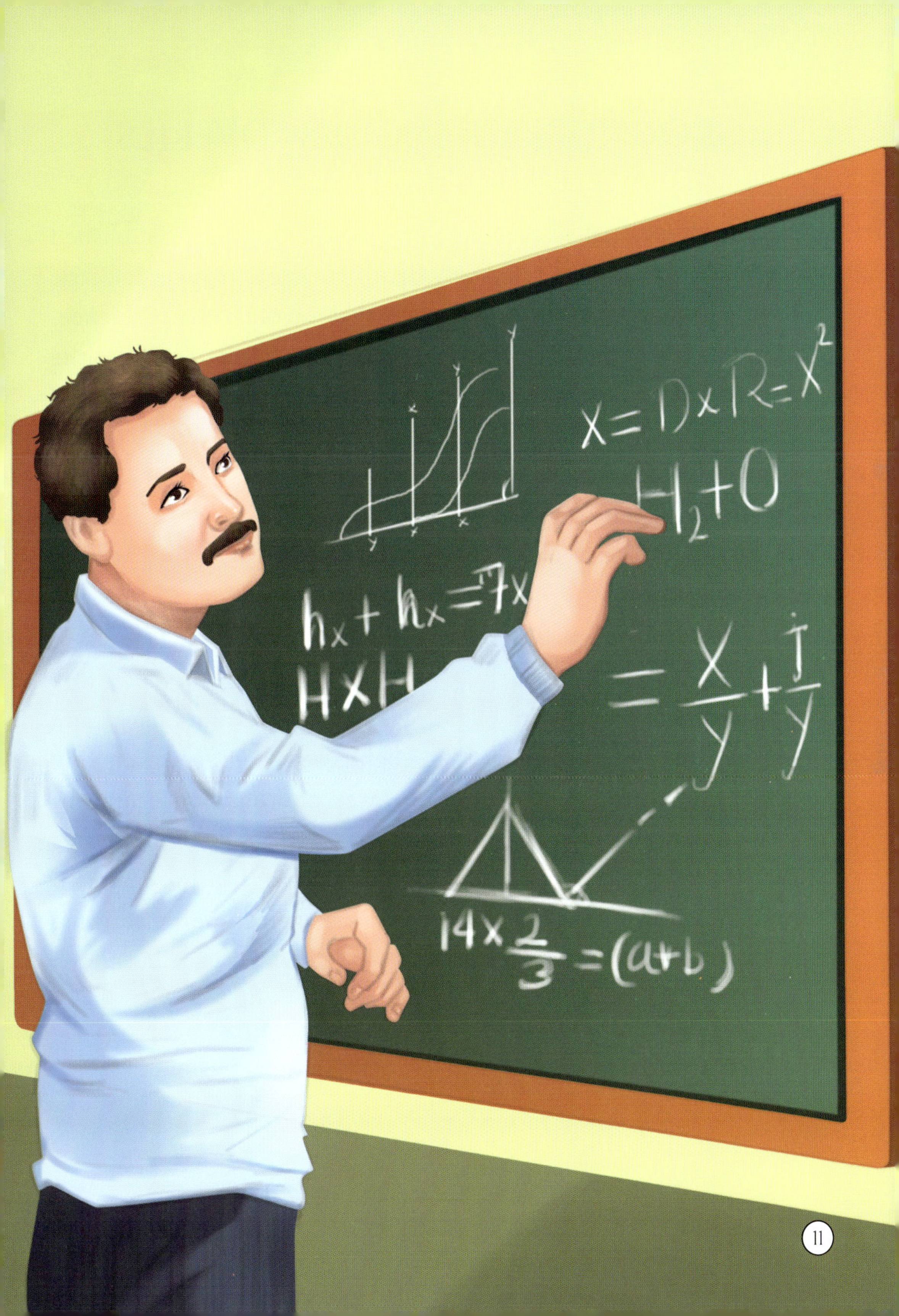
X = D x R = X²
H₂+O
hx + hx = 7x
H x H
= X/y + j/y
14 x 2/3 = (a+b)

GROUNDBREAKING DISCOVERIES

The year 1905 is called the miracle year for Einstein. He published four papers on special relativity, Brownian motion, photoelectric effect, and mass-energy equivalence that revolutionized science. His ground-breaking discoveries brought him to the notice of the larger scientific community.

In 1909, Einstein was appointed as a professor at Zurich, and the Professor of Theoretical Physics at Prague. In 1914, he became the director at the Kaiser Wilhelm Physical Institute. In 1933, he took the position of Professor of Theoretical Physics at Princeton after his emigration to America.

Einstein's conception of light was both revolutionary and magnificent. He explained that, light was composed of tiny high-energy group of particles known as photons. According to photoelectric effect, when an electromagnetic radiation such as light hits a metal surface, it causes the electrons in the metal to eject. Electrons ejected in this process are called photoelectrons. This concept of photoelectric effect has been widely used in various electronic devices.

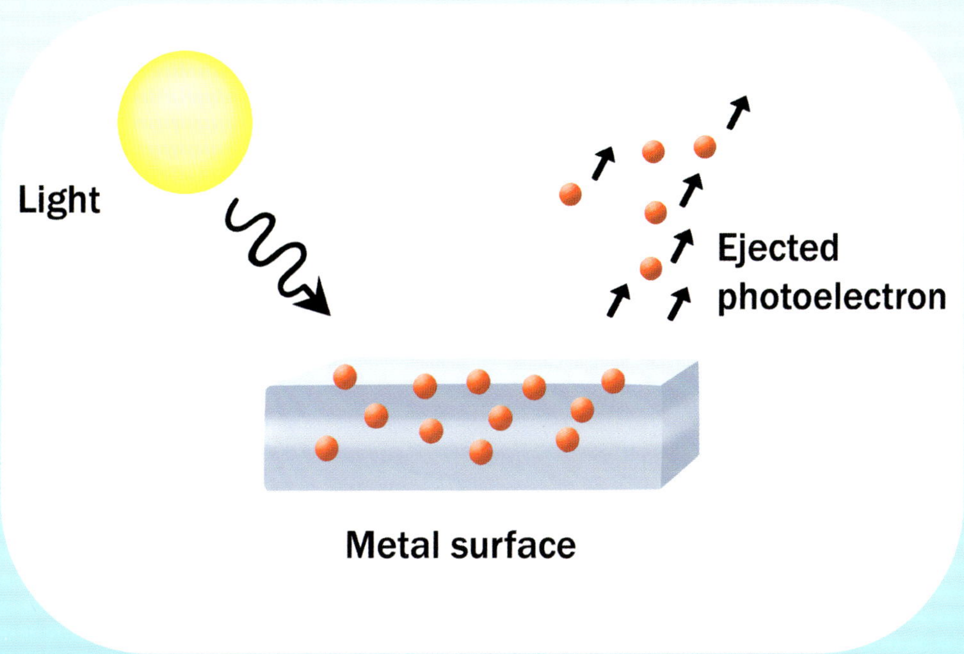
Light
Ejected
photoelectron
Metal surface

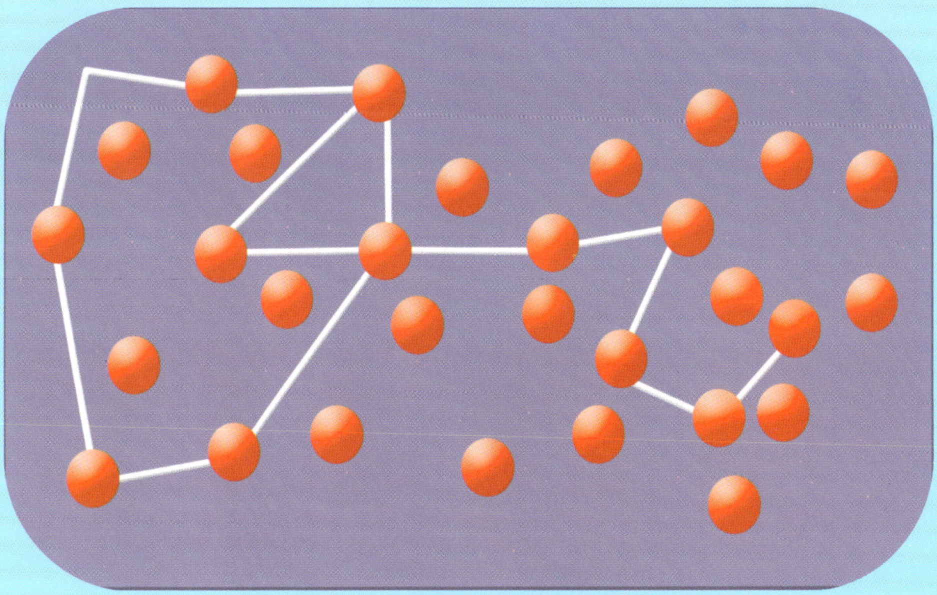

Brownian motion

Einstein's paper on 'Investigations on the Theory of the Brownian Movement,' adds to the discovery of Robert Brown's observation, that small particles of dust move randomly on the surface of water. This he called was due to the property of the liquid. Einstein described this motion with the help of mathematical equations which paved the way for a new area of research in the field of fundamental physics.

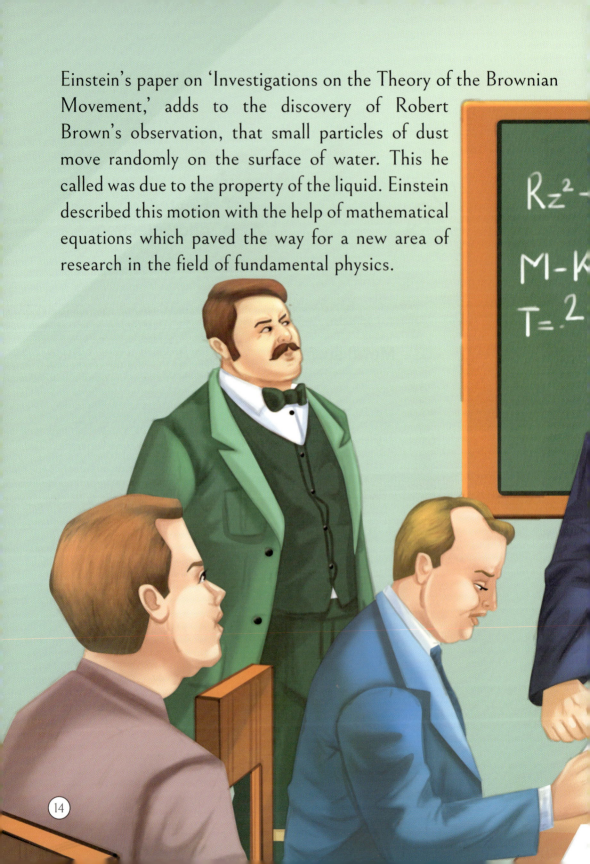

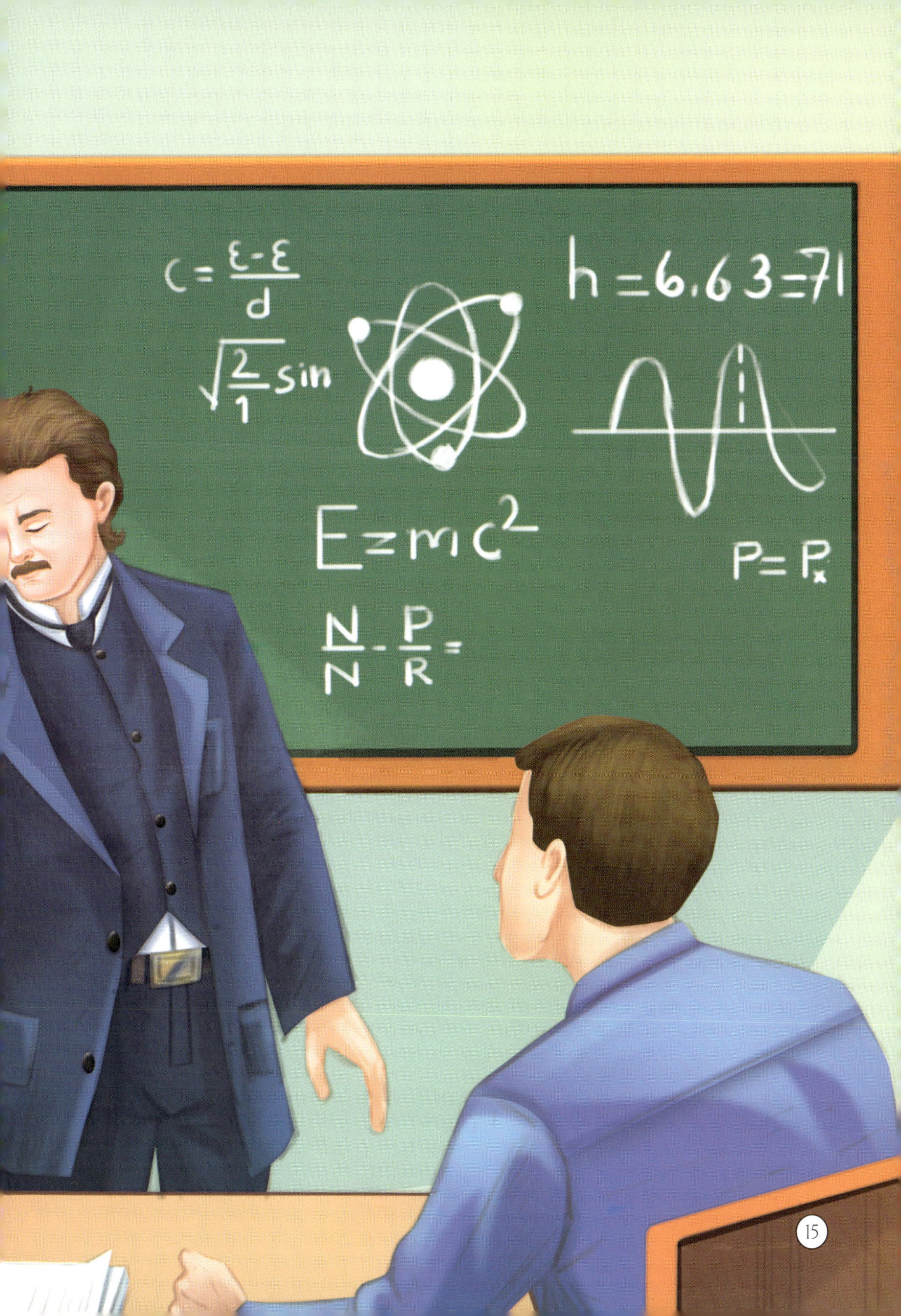
E=mc2

Einstein proposed his theory of special relativity in his paper 'On the Electrodynamics of Moving Body.' The theory of special relativity states the relationship between space and time. This theory replaced the conventional notion of time being universal and absolute to being dependent upon the reference frame and spatial position. This theory served as the the basis for Einstein's theory of general relativity in 1915.

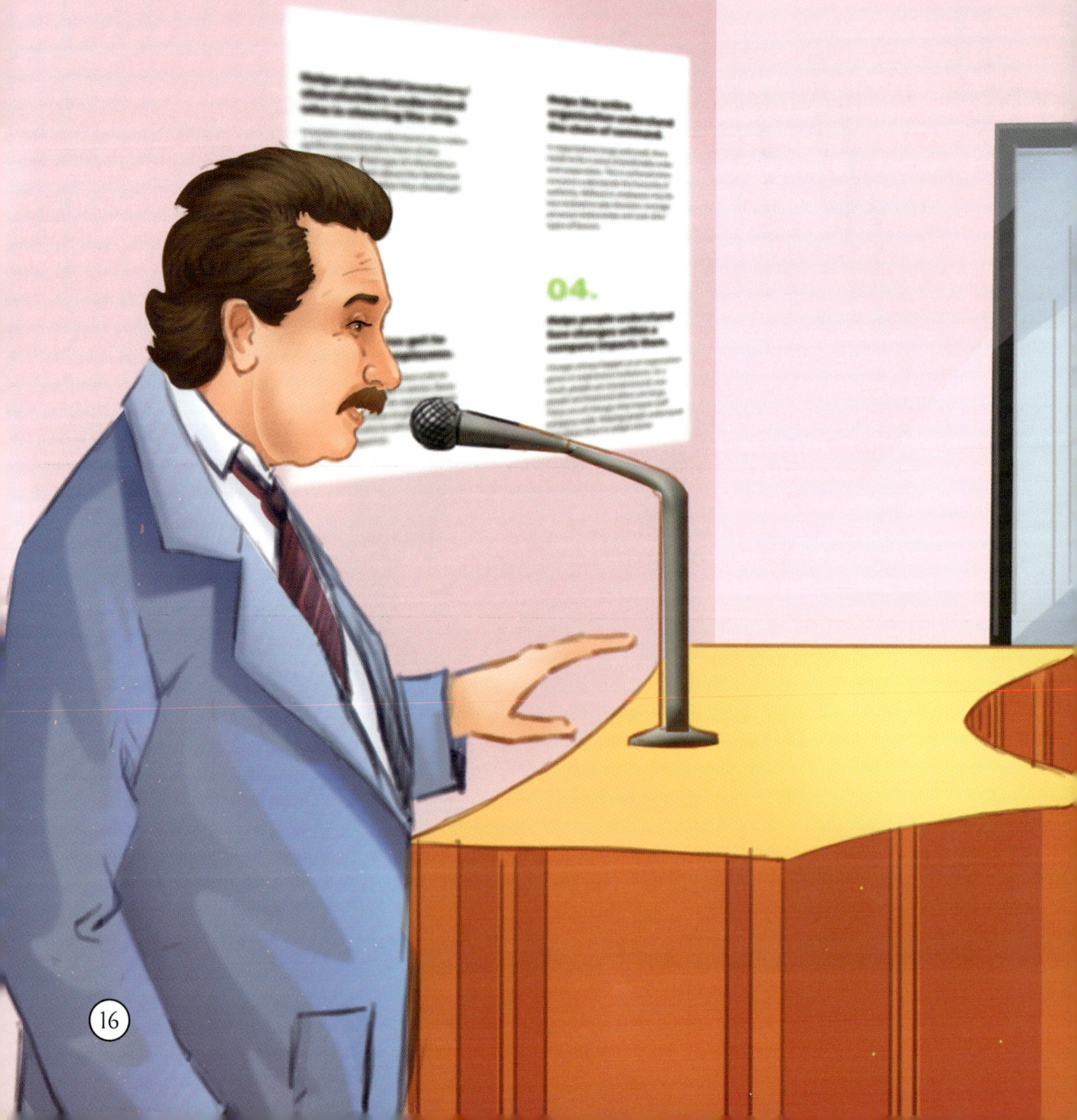
04.

Einstein's most famous equation $E = mc^2$, came from his special theory of relativity, which states that, the speed of light is always the same in vacuum. The equation also says that anything with mass has an equivalent amount of energy and vice versa. This brought a completely new understanding of the ways of the universe and expressed that mass and energy are infact the same entities which cannot be separated from each other.

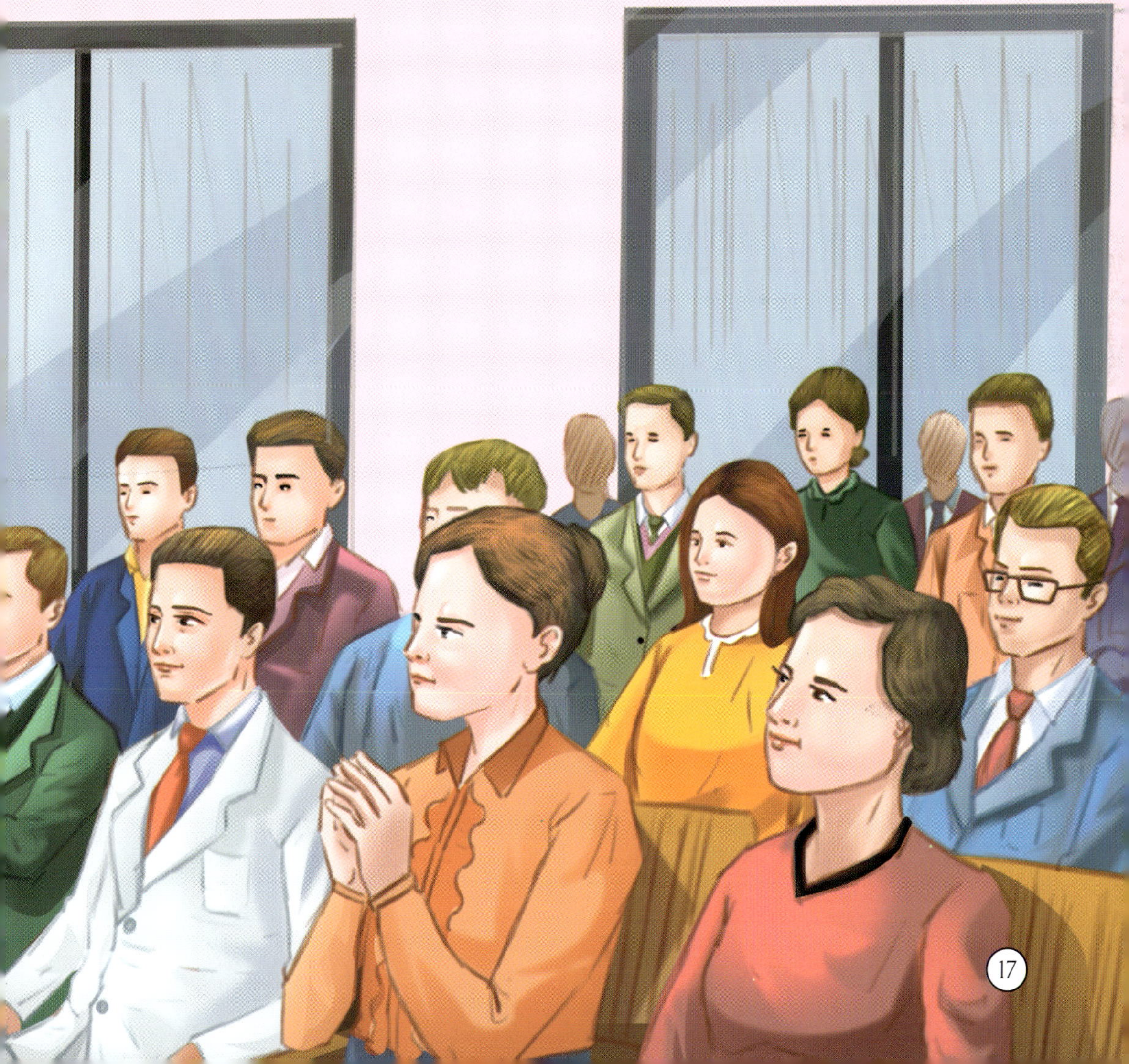

Expanding upon his special theory, Einstein proposed the general theory of relativity. In his theory, Einstein showed that space and time were in fact intertwined. It states that the force of gravity that attracts objects to one another, is nothing but a curving and warping of space. The more massive the object, the more it warps the space around itself. For example, it may appear that the planets rotate around the sun due to the pull of the sun's gravity but instead, the laws of space and time around the sun dictate the movement of Earth and other planets around it.

The theory also states that, time moves slowly when the gravity is stronger. For this reason, clocks move slower at the sea levels compared to the mountain top. Einstein's general theory of relativity has many far-reaching consequences and has been used to explain several phenomena even centuries after its discovery.

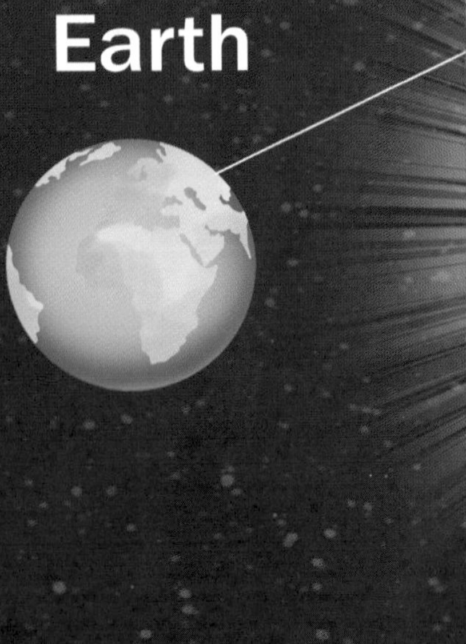
Earth

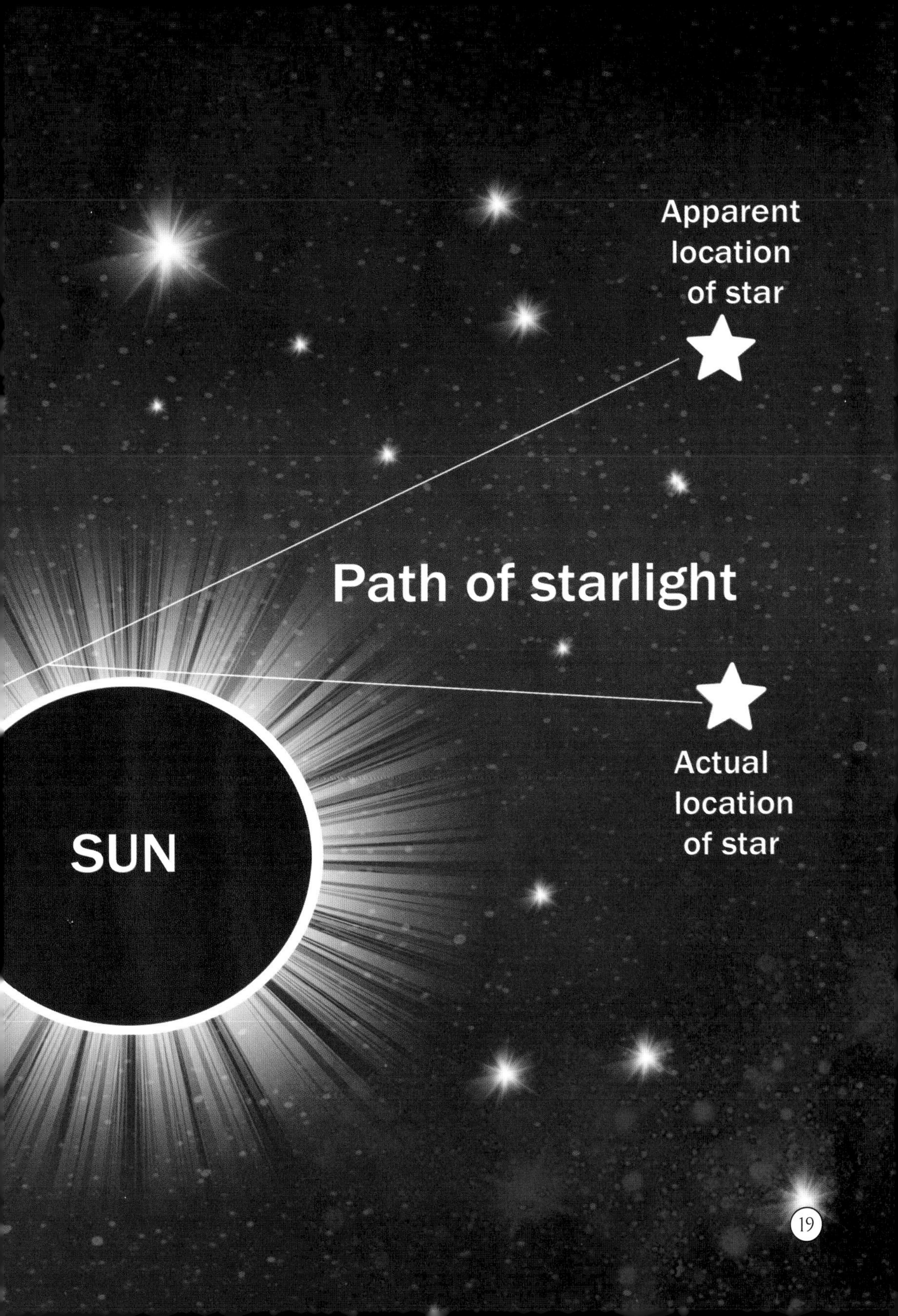
Apparent location of star
Path of starlight
Actual location of star
SUN

Einstein's theory explained the relative motion of planets and the bending of light from distant stars and galaxies. It also predicted that the universe is continuously expanding, as later proved by astronomer Edwin Hubble in 1929. The theory also predicted existence of black holes and the gravitational waves.

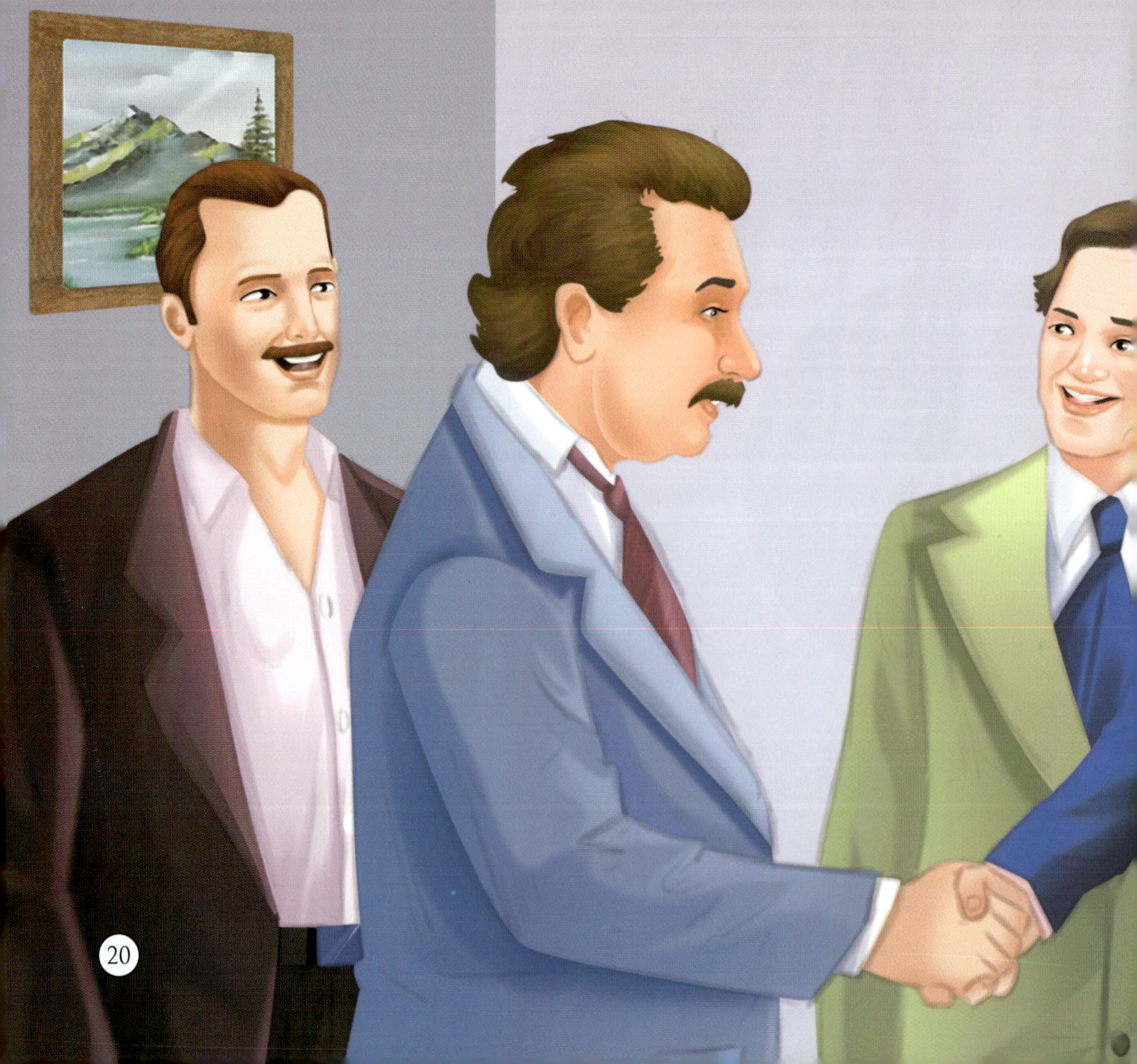

On 29 May 1919 Sir Arthur Eddington led an expedition to the Island of Príncipe off the west coast of Africa to observe a total solar eclipse. During the eclipse, when the moon blocked the sunlight for the stars to be visible near the sun, it was observed that the position of the stars appeared displaced. This displacement was due to the bending of light on the curved space around the sun caused by the gravity. The scientists were astounded with the results as it proved that Einstein's theory was in fact true.

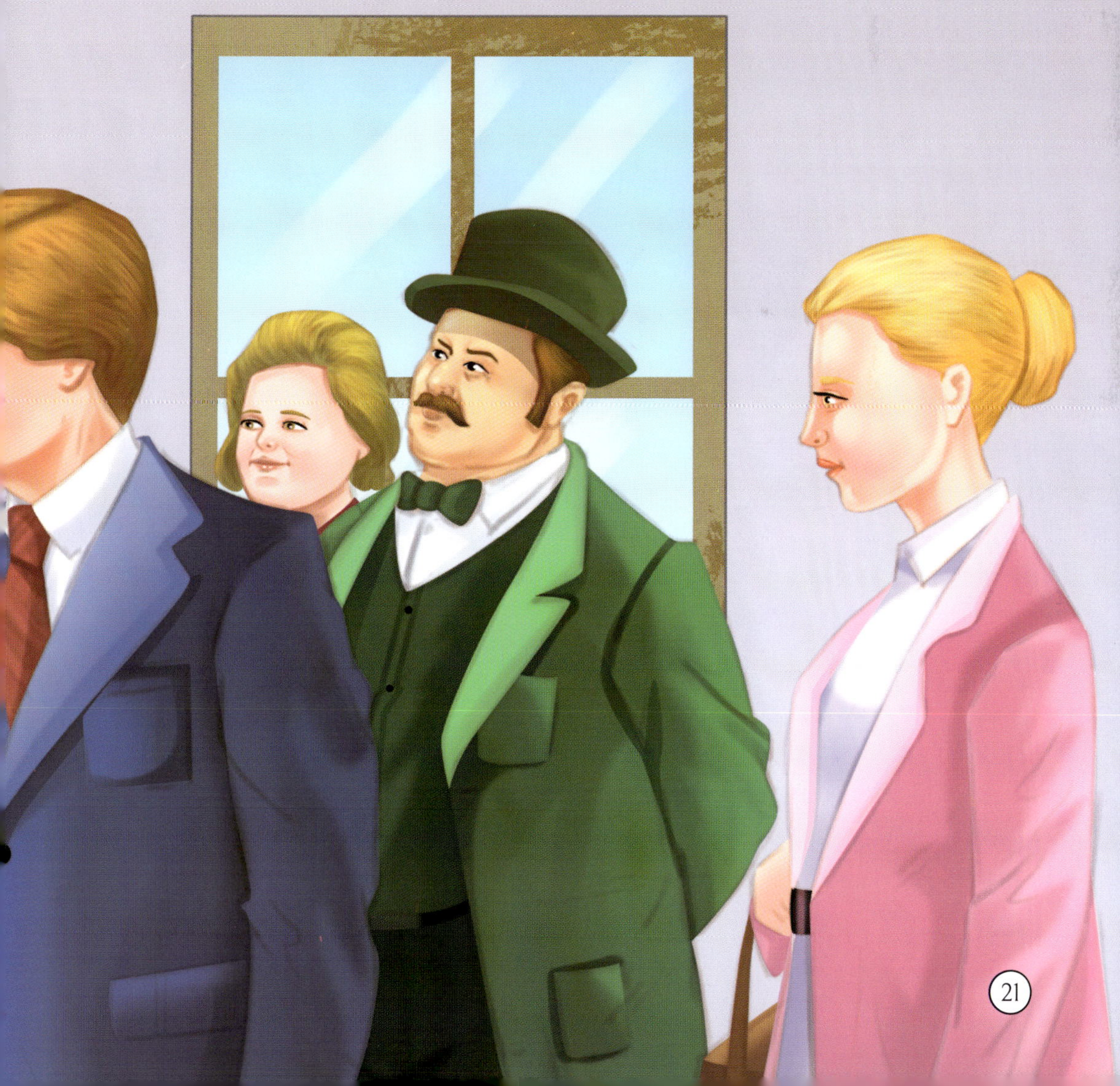

TRAGEDY OF LIFE

As Einstein made name for himself in the field of sciences, his marriage was falling apart. He spent most of his time away from home traveling and addressing conferences and imparting lectures. While at home the couple would always argue about their meagre income and their children. As their fights became regular, it became more obvious that they were falling apart.

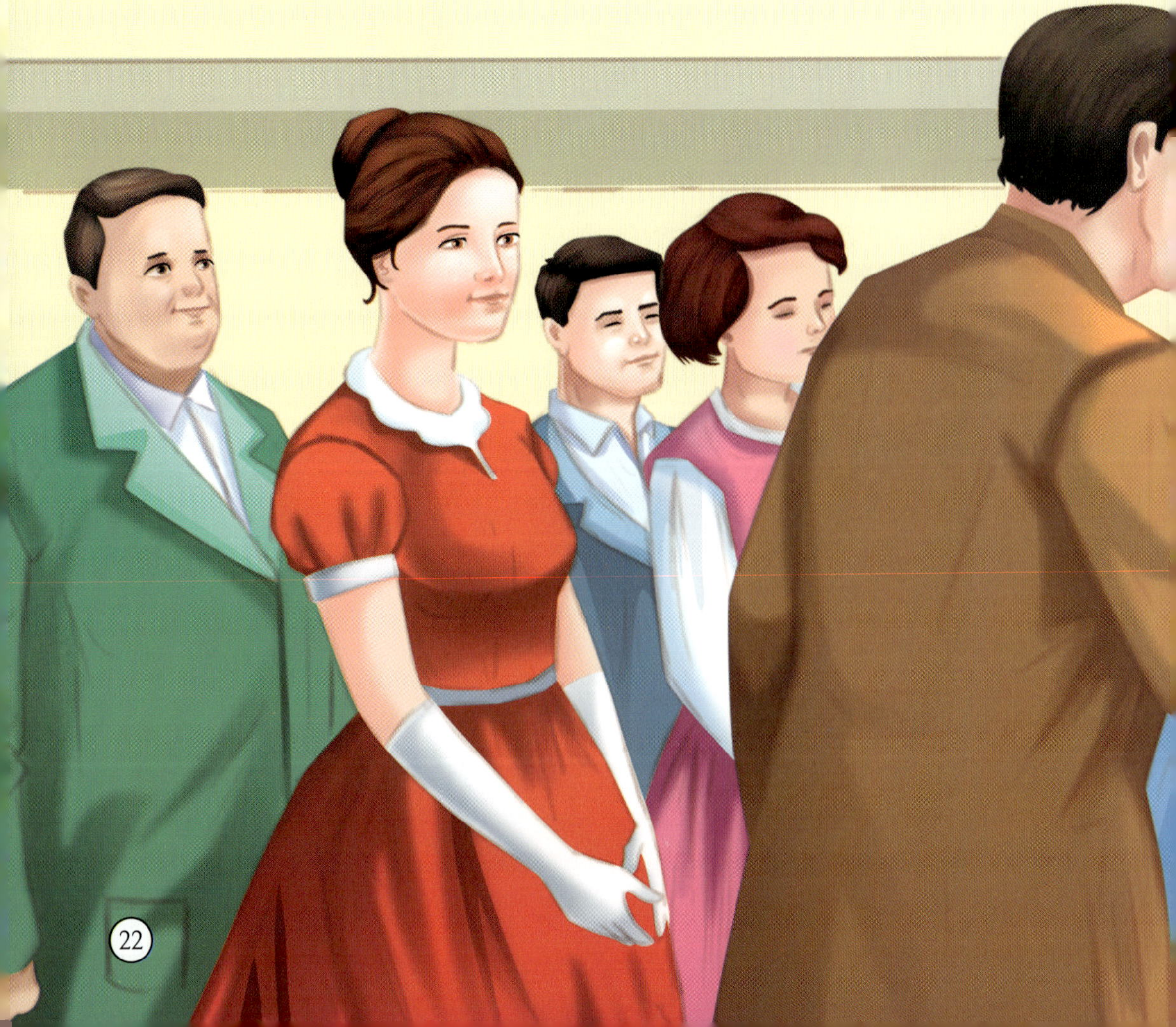

Einstein divorced Mileva in 1919, as a divorce settlement he agreed to give away the money which he will get, if he wins any Nobel Prize in the future. Later Einstein married to Elsa Löwenthal in 1919 and they moved to US in 1933. Elsa died later in 1936 due to severe heart and kidney ailments.

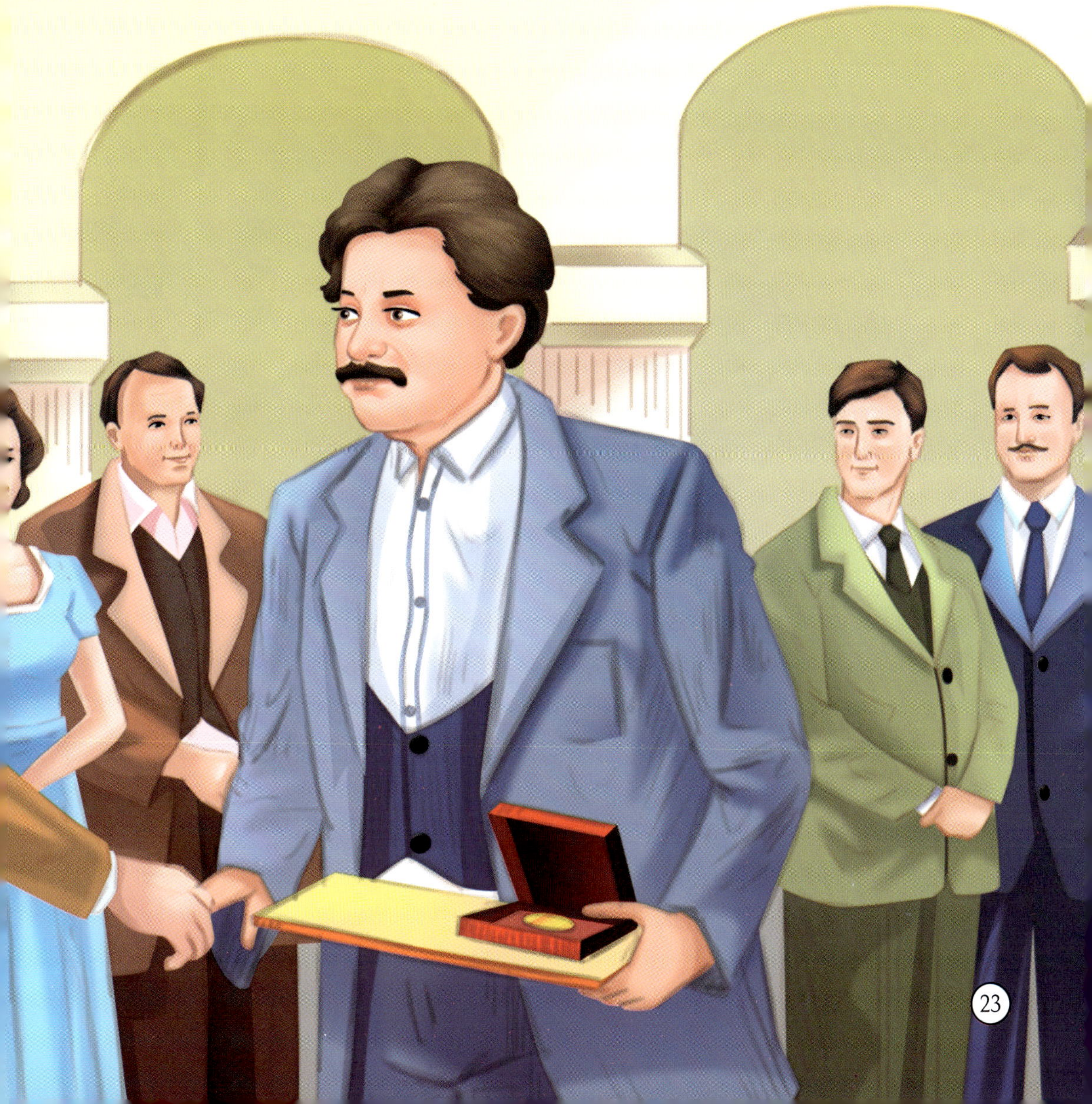

TRIUMPHS AND TRIBULATIONS

Einstein won the Nobel Prize in 1921 for the discovery of photoelectric effect and for his services in the field of Theoretical Physics. Later, Einstein was elected as a foreign member of the Royal Society and won the Copley Medal of the Royal Society in 1925 and Franklin Medal from Franklin Institute in 1935.

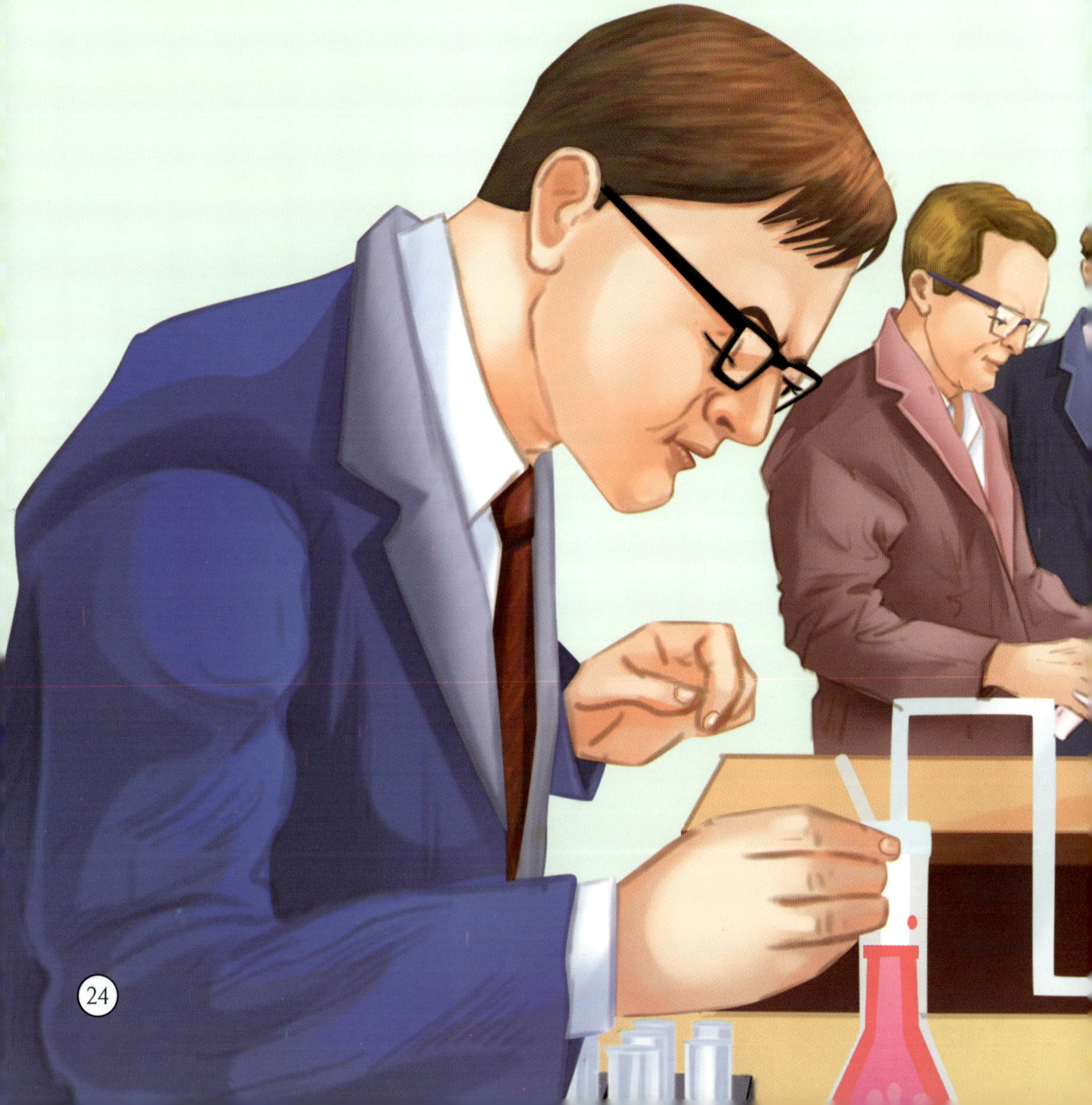

Despite the difficulties in his personal life, Einstein went ahead and earned several honorary doctorate degrees in the field of science, medicine and philosophy from many prestigious universities. He received many more awards and honors in recognition of his work and toured Europe, America and far East to deliver lectures and head several conventions and conferences.

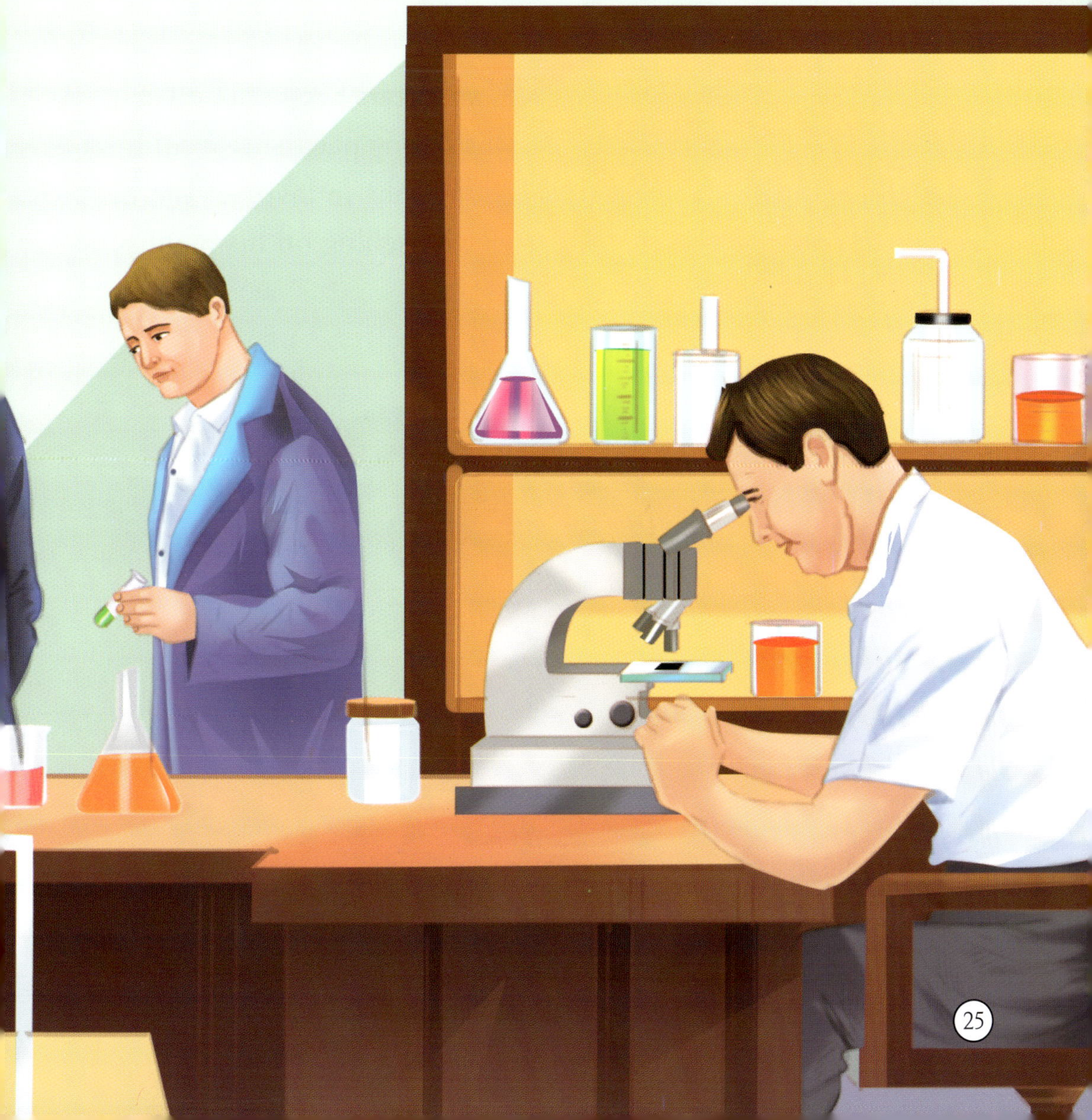

MANHATTAN PROJECT

During World War II, Einstein worked on Navy weapon systems. In 1939, he signed a letter addressed to President Franklin D. Roosevelt to alert him of the possible German nuclear attack and in response to it, the US government set to prepare their own nuclear arsenal.

This led to the start of the US Manhattan Project. Einstein was not part of this project because of his strong pacifist stance. During the war he made huge monetary donations in favor of the people affected by the atrocities of the war, by selling off his manuscripts that were worth millions of dollars!

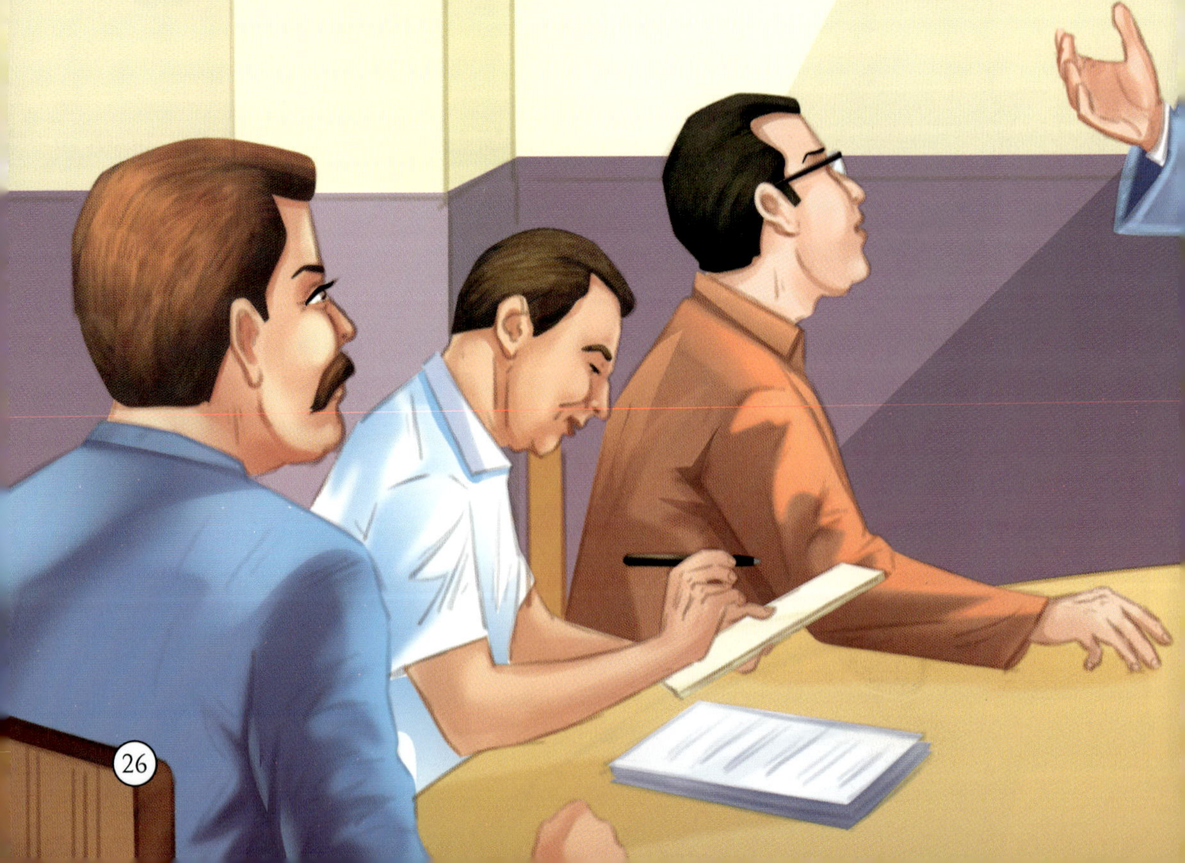

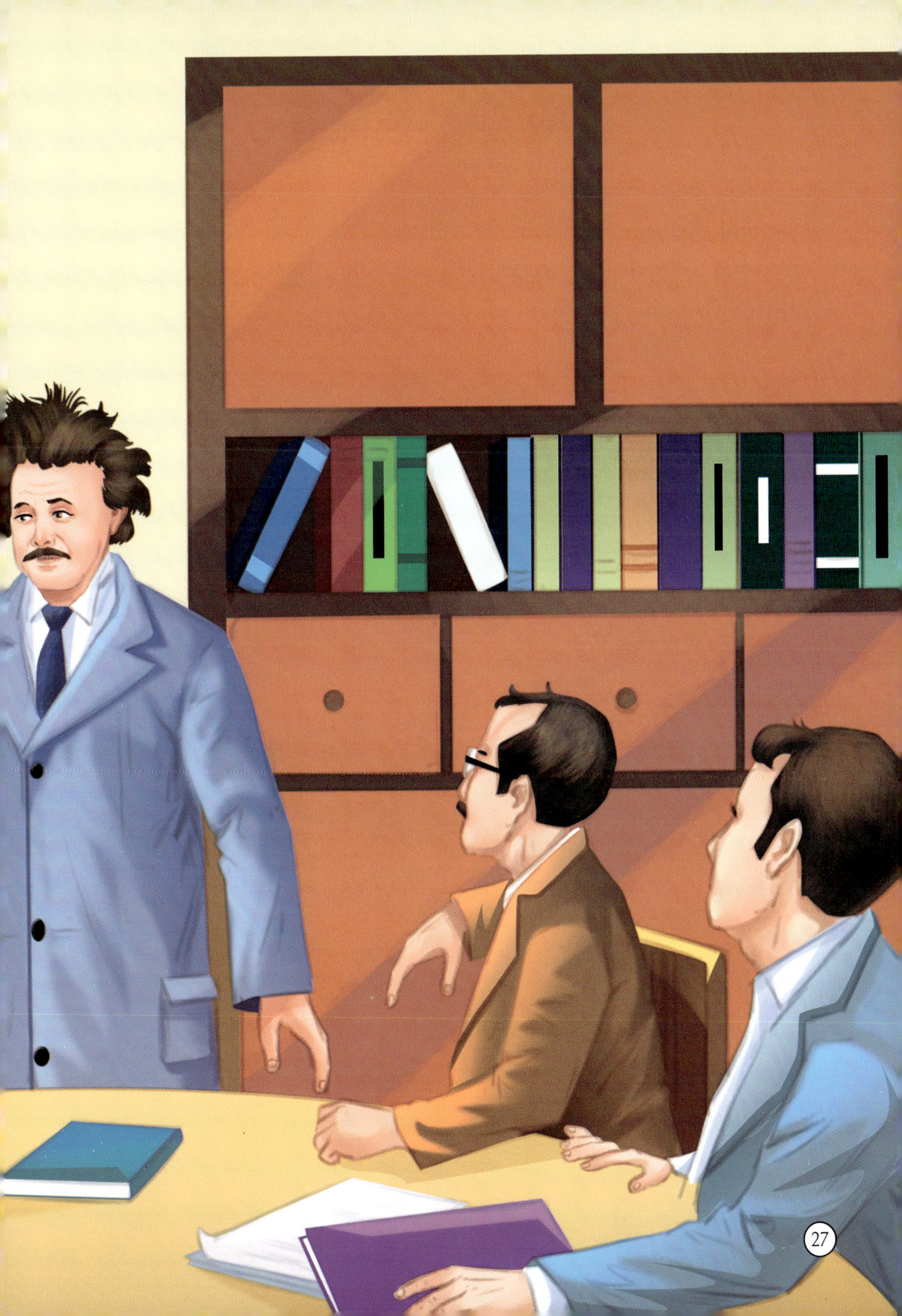

NEAR THE END

Einstein died on 18 April 1955 at the age of 76. He suffered from abdominal aortic aneurysm. He was admitted to the hospital but refused to undergo any kind of surgery.

He wanted to leave the world gracefully and did not want to artificially prolong his life. He ardently believed that he had already done his part and it was now time to go.

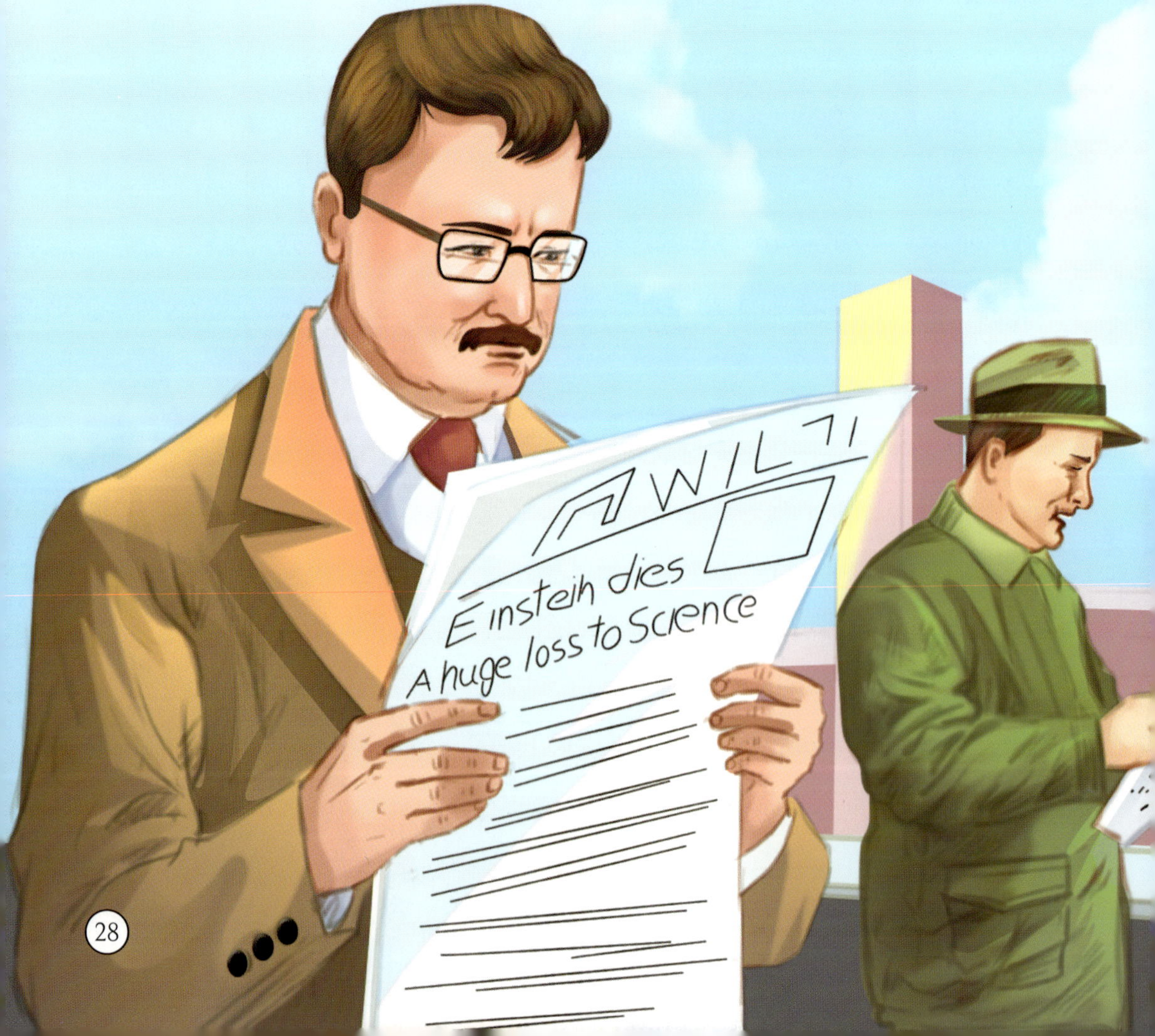
Einstein dies
A huge loss to Science

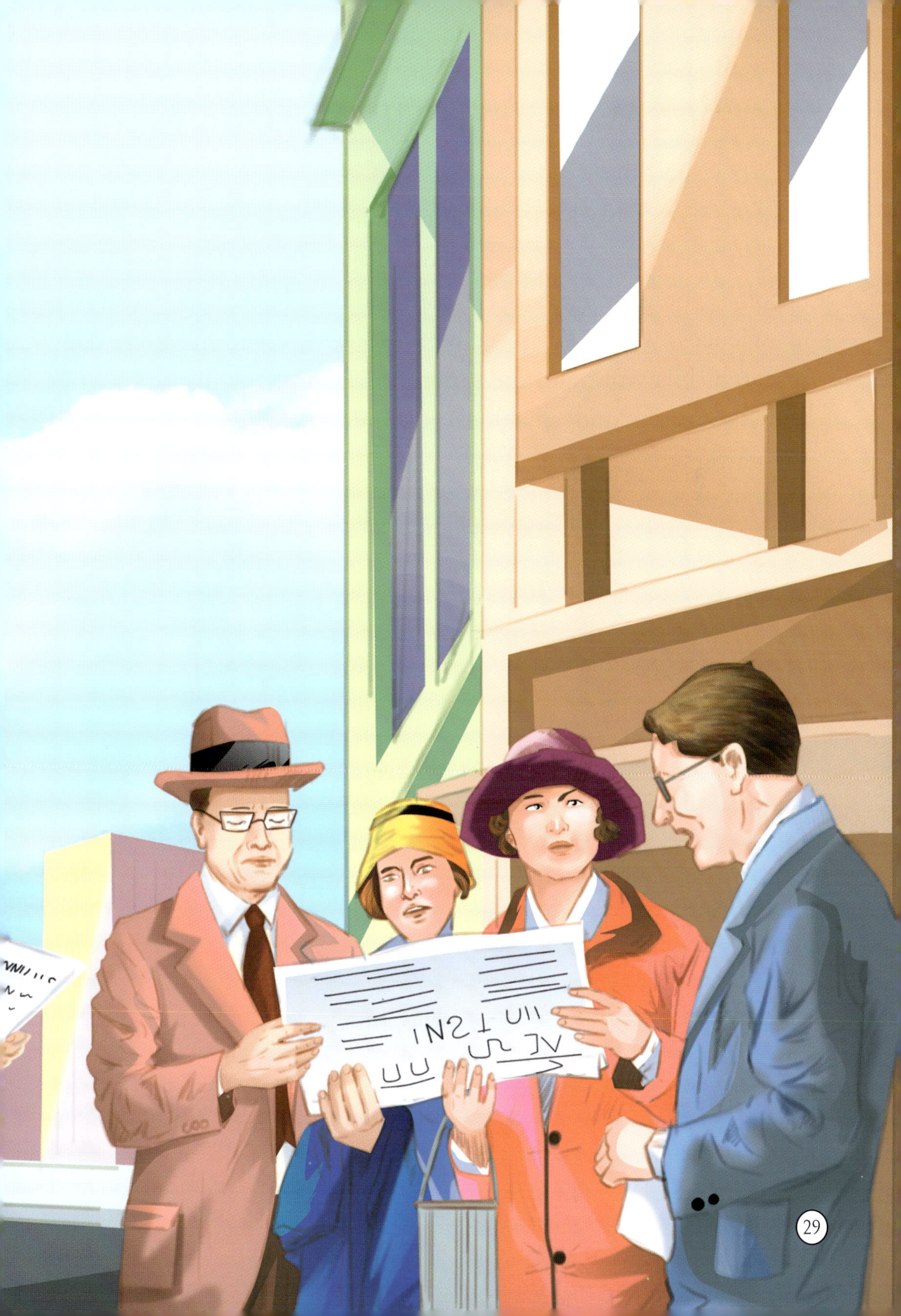

LEAVING BEHIND A LEGACY

Einstein is one of the most influential scientists to walk on the face of earth, so was his brilliance that the name Einstein has become synonymous with the word genius. He brought revolution in sciences with his incredible discoveries and path-breaking research. His work laid the groundwork for many future theories and discoveries and changed the fundamental understanding of the universe.

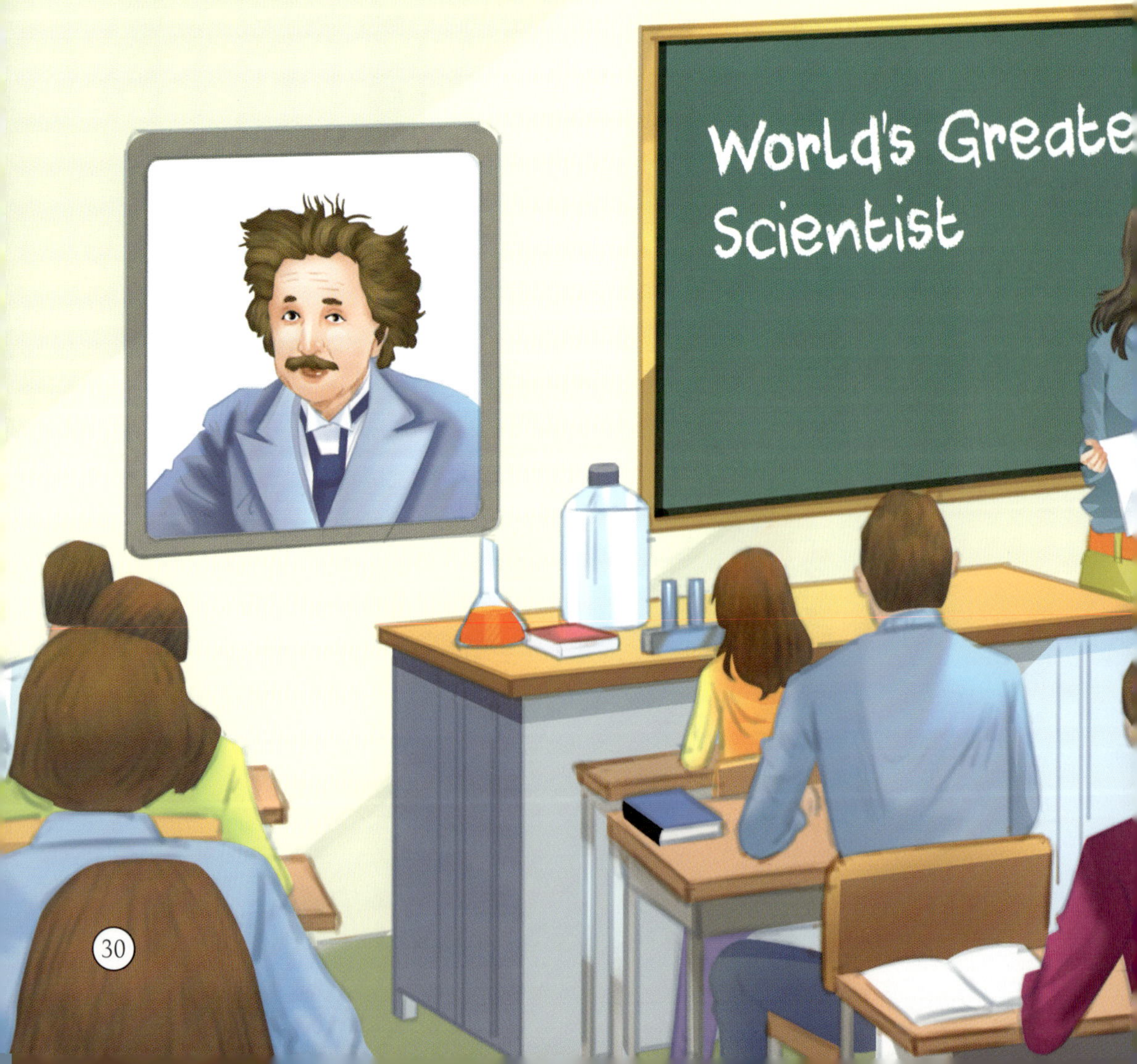
World's Greate
Scientist

He worked towards the upliftment of marginalized communities and spoke in the favor of freedom, and human rights. He worked towards the nuclear disarmament and fought against the nuclear bombs and tests. Even his last act was for the sake of humanity, just days before his death, he signed the Russell-Einstein Manifesto, warning the world about the dreadful consequences of a nuclear war.

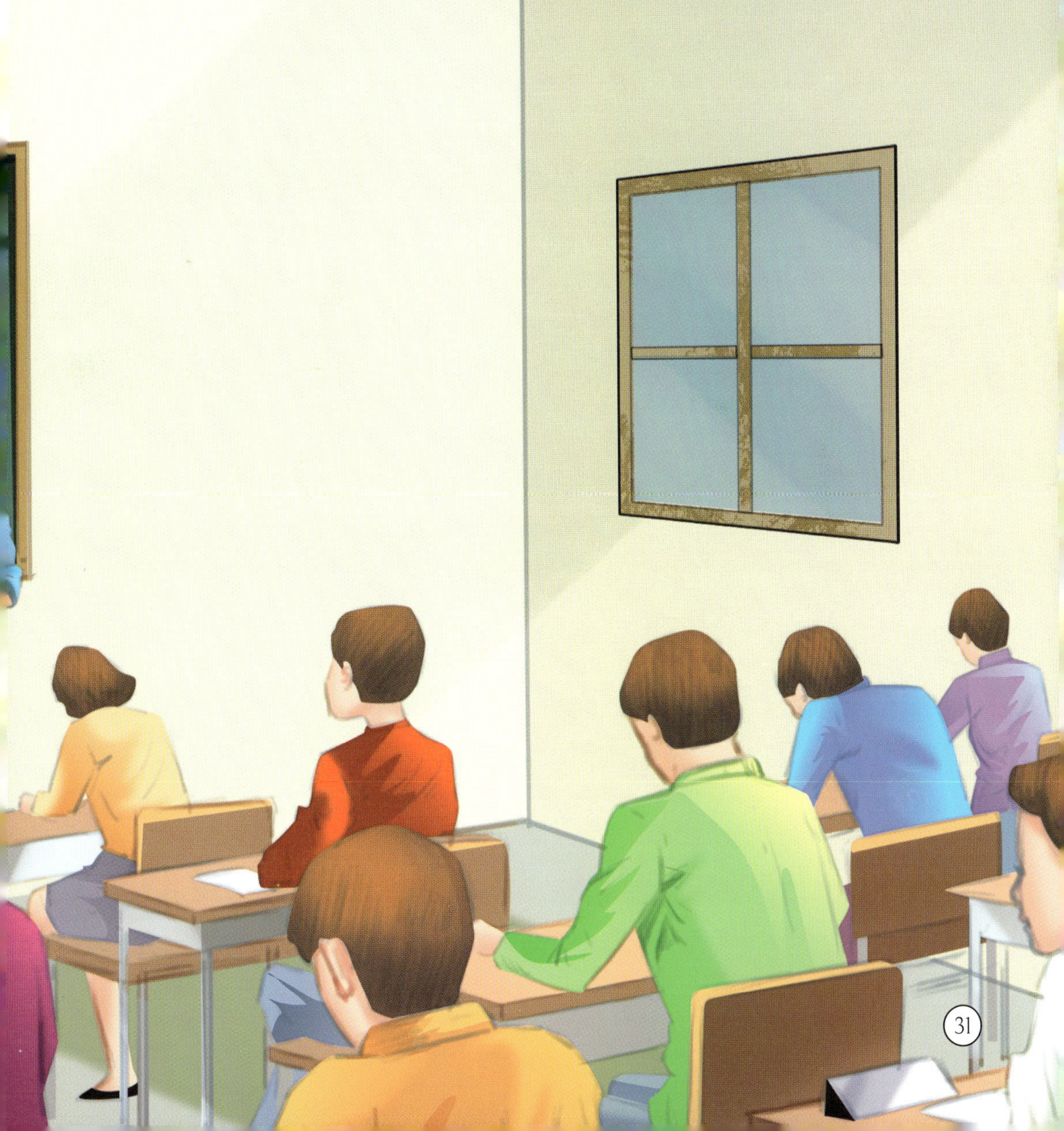

1879 : Albert Einstein is born in Ulm, Germany

1888 : Einstein enters the Luitpold-Gymnasium

1896 : Admits to the Swiss Federal Polytechnic School, Zurich

1901 : Officially becomes a Swiss citizen

1902 : Einstein is hired as a patent officer

1903 : Married to Mileva

1905 : Einstein completes his paper on quantum theory;
Paper on Brownian motion is published;
Einstein's paper on the special theory of relativity is
published

1909 : Appointment as Professor of Theoretical Physics at
Zurich University

1919 : Einstein and Mileva get divorce;
Einstein marries his cousin Elsa in Berlin;
A solar eclipse allows the scientists to observe
phenomena predicted by Einstein's general relativity
theory

1921 : Wins the Nobel Prize for his discovery of photoelectric
effect

1936 : Elsa Einstein dies

1939 : Signs a letter to President Franklin D. Roosevelt urging
the acceleration of atomic bomb development

1955 : Einstein dies